LANGUAGE HAS NO WORDS

Praise for *Language Has No Words*

"The simple, humble Haiku form achieves impressive variegation in this delicate yet full-blooded collection of apercus and epiphanies about love, death, birth, sex, grief, nature, art, and the human spirit. In Marialicia González's hands (and ear and eye and heart), a mere seventeen syllables can—and frequently does—contain a whole world."

—SHAWN LEVY, *New York Times* bestselling
author and poet

"In this beautiful haiku collection, Marialicia González distills messy emotions, like forgiveness and grief, into shimmering truths. Her poems transport the reader beyond words into an understanding she births: 'I am pregnant with story/One.word. at.a.time.' At once demanding and delighted, her work encompasses an emotional range from ecstasy to anger: 'Grief I am your bitch/….Fuck me and be gone.' Read this collection and find a harmony to fill your day."

—KATE GRAY, author of *For Every Girl*

Language Has No Words

MARIALICIA GONZÁLEZ

BisonButterflyPress.com

LANGUAGE HAS NO WORDS
BisonButterflyPress.com

Book design by Vinnie Kinsella, Paper Chain Book Publishing Services

ISBN: 979-8-9863384-0-8
eISBN: 979-8-9863384-1-5

Library of Congress Control Number: 2022911421

to my daughter

*may your creative curiosity & spark
always be guiding forces in your life*

PREFACE

It's hard to know when exactly my love for Haiku began. Was it in fourth grade when I wrote my first Haiku about a shamrock? Or maybe when in my mid-twenties I wanted to make a practice of noticing small and simple moments that I otherwise would have passed over. My dear friend Stephanie and I, she in Manhattan and me in Boston, wrote Haiku on postcards or any other acceptable rectangular shaped item that the postal service would accept, and mailed two Haiku per week to one another. We did this for almost two years and accumulated Haiku that spoke to our challenges, fears, broken hearts, sexy dates, and every day ramblings:

A tiny zigzag
Makes a path up my mirror
It's a ladybug

Going on ebay
For the first time to sell my stuff
Someone wants my goods

Or the time I read about a Cuban refugee who was found floating in the sea:

A Cuban dying
As he floats along the sea
He found his freedom

What I know for sure is that Haiku has been a life-long love. A simple and honest form that contains only 17 syllables per poem, and within that container, I find the space for deep reflection and insight.

What you will experience in the poems that follow, are highlights of a well lived life. These poems aren't for everyone. Likely just you and me. They are arranged purposefully, to offer you the space and breath to be with each one at a time. They don't follow strict Haiku rules. Once after teaching a Haiku class during a poetry festival, I was informed by the director that "maybe you shouldn't call these poems Haiku since you don't follow the rules." That may have been the best compliment I've ever gotten!

What rules these poems do follow are my rhythms and musings. My perception of the world; my point of view. As a trilingual, first generation, Cuban-American woman, I move through life with color and song. I dream brightly and think in the syllabic rhythm of 5-7-5.

In 2015, I was living through one of the darkest times of my life. My mother's death, heartbreak, and loss of community and time, shattered my heart in ways I had no words for. The darkness was deep and all encompassing. I was losing faith in life and in myself.

It had been years since writing my last Haiku, but Haiku had remembered me; and in that darkness, Haiku whispered,

I will contain you
Hold and house you in your grief
Write it out through me

And so I did. I wrote it all - the dark, the gross, the howling pain. I let myself express all of it, within the contained fire of 5-7-5.

And then Haiku's next invitation came:

If Haiku could speak
Mine would say, "Give me a wall!
I want to sing.... LOUD"

I searched and searched for who might "let" me paint my Haiku on their wall. I felt deflated and wondered how in the world I would realize this calling. Haiku wisdom whispered again..... I could write the Haiku on a piece of paper and tape them to city street walls.

And thus was born Haiku graffiti and my entrance into the street art community.

The journey continued when Haiku told me, "I want to be worn..." Um, okay, I thought. But how? (again Haiku showed me the way) ~ a whisper from a friend, "what about burning them into leather?" Which led to my love for and learning how to do leatherwork and burn my poems into bags and cuffs.

This book, this treasure, you hold in your hands, is what Haiku's next step is. Haiku seeded deeply within me and waited patiently, while I edited this book, nine months pregnant. While I birthed and mothered my newborn child. While I got on my feet as a single parent; and four years after my first meeting with my editor, here we are.

My hope is that these poems accompany you through your days and nights. That you feel the allyship and wonder, for yourself and your life, that I have felt having these tiny and meaningful poems in me. Thank you for investing in yourself and my dream.

And here are some BIG thanks for those who have walked with me and helped formed this book:

- My dear friends and family who appreciated my grief and were comfortable with my darkness, so Haiku and I could find each other once again.
- My friend Shawn, who sat with me in a coffee shop in 2017 explaining all the possible ways to go from having hundreds of poems to a collection. He told me, "you're one of the ones who goes from ideas to getting things done." Your confidence in me has truly been a buoy.

- Christopher Luna, my editor, who took my poems seriously & arranged them beautifully.
- The Portland, Oregon writing community ~ where I found writers' tables, open mics, rickety stages, tiny rooms, and comfy couches to share my words, heart, and tears. My love for you is so deep in my bones, you are part of my DNA.
- The Grief Rites Community ~ my kin, my loves, my trusted allies.
- The Portland, Oregon street art community - you validated my artistry. You took joy in my words. You showed up at my art show. You loved me.
- My daughter, my child, my Star. The incarnation of a dream that is a living and breathing reminder that I am Magic.

Awake

You are the Sun. Shine.
Wake up to all that is you
And forget the rest

3:47
before the bird songs begin
I've woken, wondering

The Sun still sleeping
But Shakti keeps me awake
Life force spiraling

Ready for the dawn
I let the dark wake me up
With bright light and song

Heaven's gate opens
Drawing us into wonder
The beasts surrender

I am a jungle
The wild in me strikes the tame
Waking up the dawn

Soaring like Angels
Eagles fly into the sun
I am one of them

Light streams from Above
I am the Weight of the Sun
Scorching the Darkness

Star light, star brighter
You're the first star of this night
Shining into me

I stand here with you
Amidst the wild ride of life
Sturdy and strong willed

When light walks with dark
The answer is always yes
I rest and take flight

Curiosity

Curiosity
keeping all the doors open wide
my heart and my soul

Your blue eyes shining
Gleaming with tears, watching me
While I'm watching you

Flame to the fire
From the drop to the ocean
Mighty perfection

Painting a mystery
Bleeding orange into red
White is the border

Swirling through the sky
Journey up, journey into
Hopeful horizons

Arms raised touching sky
Mudra breathing in repose
Happiness sated

I've no words today
Quietude fills up my space
Spiraling silence

Spiraling Shakti
Drawing up the life forces
Volcano erupts

Flames & flowers bloom
In the cavern of my chest
I fly away blue

Home to so many
Grounded deep into the earth
Away from the Light

Rugged & textured
Standing in gentle repose
Majestic. Mighty.

Where green meets the blue
And shadows of clouds float by
You so softly sway

Simple is your reach
Soaring toward the Skyward Sun
Rooted in the earth

Spiraling Awake
Through the crashing waves of Sea
Salty air so sweet

Sand reflects the Sky
Everything is Everything
Even nothingness

Magic & Mystery
Is happening all around
Watch for it closely

Suspended cloud forms
Holding up my dreams for me
I show up for them

Tears immediate
Sunshine in my morning tea
Streams in from the sky

Old hopes arising
Reminding me to look up
Or downward instead

Wisdom

Bye bye old longings
Hello fresh awakenings
Happy to greet you

What is jealousy
A lack of forgiving me
Or forgiving you

Words are my witness
Sometimes only words can see me
When even I doubt myself

In weakness there's strength
In boldness, revelation
The quiet wakes us

Words as protection
Revelations as mystery
Understanding things

Stepping into the next right
And leaving behind all the wrongs
Mountains speak my name

Being loved by tea
Warm liquid medicine, steam…
Rising with my mood

Love is the witness
And gratitude the journey
Divine and Holy

The spell is broken
I've collected myself back
And now, the soaring

Sitting and sipping
A wizard in my tea cup
Howling winds outside

Tea speaks in silence
Quietly evoking trust
Until the next breath

Laughing leaves of love
Lean toward me as I rest
In flows the sweetness

Lessons from the leaf
Speak to me as I sip
Wisdom emerges

Electricity
Bursts from within, creating
You, inside of me

Words swimming through me
I am pregnant with story
One.word.at.a.time

Red calls out my name
And in the darkness whispers
"you are not enough"

In a fit of life
white brings sweet calm to the red
Changing everything

We all come from her
And from his coming to her
Precious Mother love

Dark as the Night Sky
Her eyes look at me & say
I.am.really.here.

Rising

If haiku could speak
Mine would say, "Give me a wall!
I want to sing, Loud!"

It isn't what's said
But what's spoken through the heart
Language has no words

I, an open book
Will read from my pages free
A Phoenix rising

Marialicia
The name my mama gave me
I'm taking it back

Smiling eyes reveal
The heart in your words to me
It's all in the words

What will matter most
When your heart stops its beating?
Do you know you're loved?

Becoming brand new
Awakening to myself
Floating through darkness

Understanding truth
Misunderstanding all else
Where did the map go?

If there was no shame
What would you say or do now
Would you spread your wings?

Your name transcends time
Swirling through the wishing well
Boundless as the sun

The ones who back off
Were never the ones for you
They are the windstorm

The skin that is me.
Beautiful. Bountiful. Free.
Awake. Ecstasy.

Hot mess family
How do we come out alive?
Forgiveness is key

Love

The search that leads me
Opens to discovery
The starlight twinkles

Rivers flowing through
The source of my pure wetness
All because of you

When you die, come back
Where were you to begin with?
Swing that open door

I am so so loved
All alone but not lonely
Awake in myself

Doug fir stands alone
On the edge of a flower
But then, don't we all?

Sweetness falls like rain
Soaking in the moonlit bed
When I wake, you smile

Eyes wide open. Stare
Sunglasses cover the blue
But I can see you

You make me smile big
I see you coming and wave
Your realness slays me

Shadows bloom as one
And the Sunshine still shines bright
Why then so much pain?

When you're in your doubt
Why not presume all the best?
Your heart knows the truth.

Your disappointments
Are for you to tango with
I can dance alone

When the heart is shut
Romance doesn't stand a chance.
Words. Just empty words.

Skyward goes my heart
Thoughts ignited by the Sun
Stillness, my one friend

You dive into me.
I, your one blue Atlantis.
A lost world once more

When it comes to time
You and I are beyond it
Soul speaks soul language

Finding your way home
Can lead to an unknown place
That is way deeper

Yes to momentum
I trust you & I know you
Give me what you've got

Opening

Lips soft, awkward tongue
Brings a new taste to my mouth
You, giving to me

Your organ enters
With swiftness and my laughter!
Love tastes so.damn.good.

Moon showers bathe us
In the sweetness of my bed
Twinkle go the stars

Rain pours on roses
Nothing can burden me now
You and I are one

Drops of you come in
To the moisture of my bed
I. give in. to. you.

Bathing in darkness
Making my way to your form
You envelop me

Tongue that knows its way
Down into my honey jar
Sweetness overflows

Fingertips that stroke
My soft mountains and valleys
Fires erupting

My flesh symphonies
Buds to mountains, to rivers
Flowing into you

Grief

Grief I am your bitch
and you my senseless lover
Fuck me and be gone

Wild like the beyond
Ashes fill my screaming soul
Where is the respite?

Oh my grief lover
You dominate me wildly
Licking and lying

Oh the ache of heart
Bearing down my burden deep
This well so very wide

Did you forgive me
From the grave do you hear me
Dust in the windstorm

Tree against the sky
You reflect back to me life
In dry death you shine

A mother's love loves
A daughter's betrayal lies
How could you forgive?

Stars twinkle at night
Satellites swerve around me
You put up a fight

Tears fall like raindrops
Will they ever change to smiles
Heart tick-tocks alone

Love is the healer
My howls no longer break me
I now stand all one

When the well is dry
Then let it be alone. Dry
No more life to give

Time

Another spark out
Or maybe she's joined the stars
Make the moments count

She speaks in roses
Three dimensional time-lapse
Breaking ocean waves

Sliding door moments
When you could have, but didn't
Don't let those stack up

Surrounded by time
Encapsulated by love
Darkness doesn't mind

Dignity and Grace
Not taught, but learned over time
Time takes its own time

Inspiration speaks
Where it leads, mystery
Magical moment

A moment in time
Has been written in the stars
And it thrives on love

Child, be an outcast
That is all I want for you
Flowers bloom. You've won

Be my gentle light
I'll be your sister moon-beam
Burning through the night

Roll into the dirt
Now roll, damn straight or sideways
Where you rise, I'll be

Sleep tight little one
Wait until the morning glow
Sunshine will return

ABOUT THE AUTHOR

The daughter of Cuban refugees, Marialicia González was raised in Miami with a value in the efficiency of love & creativity. Marialicia started writing as a child, as a way to witness herself. Poetry gave rise to her imagination and haiku, in particular, captivated her. She is a grief revolutionary. Using her 30 years of experience as a midwife, RN, social worker, minister, and artist, she has transformed the heartache of deep, personal losses to become a strong voice in the cultural shift to normalize the experience and expression of grief.

Marialicia is the founder of *Daraluz Wisdom*, where she consults with individuals and groups in bringing clarity to the childbearing years and beyond. While facilitating workshops, rituals, creating courses, and providing one-to-one consulting, she supports people in making informed, wise choices, for themselves and their loved ones. She is a spaceholder, leatherworker and hiker, a storyteller and a mother.

www.ingramcontent.com/pod-product-compliance
Lightning Source LLC
Chambersburg PA
CBHW070716130626
46553CB00005B/2015